W9-CHV-815

BrotherKeeper

by
Larry Janowski

for Maureen,

fellow traveller on the

wild and wonderful

path of poetry.

Larry Janowski
2/17/07

The Puddin'head Press
2007

Additional copies of this book
may be ordered by writing to:

The Puddin'head Press
PO Box 477889
Chicago IL 60647
708-656-4900

www.puddinheadpress.com
phbooks@compuserve.com

Cover photograph by Larry Janowski
Author's photograph by Bill Mahoney

First Edition
2007

ISBN# 978-0-9724339-5-2

Dedication

This is for my beautiful parents,
William and Elizabeth Janowski,
and for my brother Mark,
a gift since the day he was born.

Table Of Contents

BrotherKeeper

...sometimes it is necessary
to reteach a thing its loveliness,
to put a hand on its brow
of the flower
and retell it in words and in touch
it is lovely
until it flowers again from within, of self-blessing . . .

"Saint Francis and the Sow" by Galway Kinnell

BrotherKeeper

It's lots and lots of people that's been killed, just part
of day-to-day life here in the Ida B. Wells Project, looks
like, you know, a 14-story cemetery.

Lloyd Newman, 10th grade
LeAlan Jones, 11th grade

On Thursday, October 13, 1994, Eric Morse, aged five,
was dropped to his death. Derrick Morse,
his eight-year-old brother,
tried to save him. Chicago boys I never knew, who
will not let go. It's like that.

In my dreams, I do not see him fall,
a movie doll dropped for our sadistic thrill,
and I refuse even to think
of screams. But what I do keep seeing
is Derrick whip-slipping down stairs

> floor to
> > floor
> > > down
> > blurred banisters
> > > two
> > > > three
> steps at a time   down
> > > 14 floors
> > > > *my brother is*
> > *falling*
> > > is
> > > > like drowning

I came close once, flailing in a lake's mud bottom
imagining my cries would rise
in cartoon balloon bubbles to burst *Help!*
in that far blue sky water ceiling, but what saved
was not a word but a brother's hand that grabbed
dragged up to air
> > > but air cares even less
> > than water, lets you
> > slip through,
> > without even a wake
> > to mark your passing

and because Eric will not steal
candy for the ten-year-olds, they
dangle him from a 14th floor window
and Derrick grabs and gets him
until one of them bites his hand
and he has to let go
                   so
       he races
               for the stairs
     I can catch him
        I can catch
   him I can
       catch him
   I can
      be
   there
     before
   he
    hits
   the
    ground

their defense attorney said
    I don't care how big, how mean they want to be,
    five minutes and you're talking to little boys,
    and every one of them . . . they're all savable
    every one of them

except this one
falling

          14 stories

   14 flights

          14 floors

     catch

       him

Brothers At Kitty Hawk

December 16
Wind. Relentless coastal blast bending
sea grass to its knees to scratch circle
signatures in sand. Wind that sucks
the breath from your lungs, that drills
sand through gaps in flimsy cabin walls,
blows out the fire in your stove, if not
what burns in your belly. You try to sleep,
staring at your brother who stares
at blinking red stars through blue wind.

Wind that can sweep from the sky like a
stricken bird your skeleton of wires, props
and gasoline, can knock you off your feet
but cannot seem to knock a lick of sense
into your head full of dreams. What makes
you think tomorrow your Flyer will not merely
glide again, but be the first to climb
the air by its own power, by the sheer
cussedness of its noisy, smelly engine?

December 17
Words lost in engine howl and gusts at
26 knots, they clasp hands, lock eyes,
toss the coin. Wilbur runs, keeps up,
then is left behind, below, Orville's first
flight of 12 seconds. Wilbur's turn adds
20 feet, then Orville 200, and then, before
winter shuts the sky, Wilbur soars 865
feet for nearly a minute in pure air
until the winds force him down 'til spring.

They taught us to fly, the monument reads,
but they taught each other first.
On Kill Devil Hills dreamwinds still blow,
full circle for 100 years, the same winds
you ride, jet-screaming across continents
like stepping stones. This is what brothers do,
after all: breathe on coals, steady hands,
shelter dreams, take turns cheering
to keep each other aloft on the damned wind.

for my brother, Mark, who flies

Blue Angels

in this dream you are lying nearby on the floor
of our back porch like we used to do
on summer nights when we were kids
stretched out on the cool linoleum both of us
under a light sheet still stifling as a quilt
in the thick air of the South Side where
even wide open windows gave no breeze
only the smell of a caravan of cattle
trucks on 47th Street a block away headed
to the stockyards grinding gears in the dead
of night hitting the brakes at Western Avenue
so the cattle bawl their terror and stink
to where we jerk and toss in our sleep
and this woman walks up and stands
next to me and now still in the dream
I'm not a kid but the man I am and she
is still standing with a suitcase beside her—
like Blanche DuBois over-dressed and lost
and I think maybe I recognize her after all so I ask
what I can do for her but she says nothing
and I'm relieved because I don't want to anyway
but then she says there is this one thing
and I tell her I am tired of people with problems
I can't do anything about and lock the door
and say to you dead brother John that if people
are going to just walk up out of nowhere
from New Orleans right onto our porch then
even though I feel guilty . . . but if crazy people
keep coming we'll have to sleep inside even
when it's as hot as it is today and the Blue Angels
buzzed Chicago with their shock of speed and
warplay and now sweating happy crowds
are heading back home from the lakefront
and I sit with three friends at a sidewalk café
when this guy comes up tall and slim and
very dark talking loud and we realize
we'd been hearing his voice across the street
but now he's here standing next to our table reciting
in sad sentences a script he knows by heart

and kneels down *he hurt bad so I gave him 8 grams*
of pure her-o-in, yeah, but Sarge, now the kid
is dead he chokes and stands snaps-to so his shadow falls
on your long blond hair and all four of us keep sipping
coffee and tea not missing a beat of our conversations
all of us knowing the rules of nonengagement
knowing there is nothing we can do nothing
we can change nothing we can bring back
from the dead and after our little thrill
we will wake

Omen 1949

At four or five, the boy finds abandoned
blackberry brandy, purplesweet as jelly,
and downs the tumbler full. Aunts and uncles
chuckle at his reeling. They must have forgotten
that first birthday party when family tradition
set before him in his highchair throne three
seeming gifts: *If he grabs the silver dollar,*
he'll be rich for sure; the rosary beads, a priest;
the shot glass, a drunk; how they laughed
when all he missed was the money.

Sitting Up Nights

Grandpa Petra calls me in his American Slovak
Šitkumaly—his Little Shit—the laugh humming
through me, sunk in the slope of his warm lap.
I press into strong hands that rub my back
as if I am a lamp with a secret inside, and we
settle deeper into his maroon chintz chair
where he would sit alone most of the day
and night, convinced that if he lay down
he'd die in bed.
          One morning I wake to hear
my father saying to my mother, "He's gone.
In his chair." Days later, Dad burned it
in the vacant lot. The chair, I now suppose,
had been soiled by death's relaxations,
the stain of loss seeped indelibly into wood
and hemp, or maybe it held a ghost
in its arms.
          At three years old I run away
from home—trek the long block, cross
the street by myself into tall weeds,
follow the sweet smell of dead fire
to a circle where charred oak bones
still sit, spring upon the coils, taste
a cloud of ashes, ruin my clothes.

First Words

There will soon be no more priests. Their work is done.
                                    Walt Whitman, 1885

*Like priests in a town of agnostics, poets still command a
certain residual prestige. But as individual artists they are
almost invisible.*
                                    Dana Gioia, 1992

The poet at nine learns by heart his Latin verse,
not Virgil, but bits of Vulgate psalms prayed
at the foot of the altar. To the old pastor's
Introibo "I will go up,"
acolyte answers *ad deum*
qui laetificat to God "who gives joy"
juventutem meam "to my youth,"
to his boyhood of words, like those
memorized from his missal
not only his rote responses,
but words the priest must say
and names of sacred things:
starched white *purificator,* silken
chasuble, golden *ciborium*—
all untouchable and holy
as words.
         The priest at nine learns how to bow
his head at the name of Jesus uttered or heard,
to bend at the waist with grace—ignorant
of Whitman's ban on baring the head to anyone—
to confess *mea culpa mea culpa mea maxima culpa*
"my fault my fault my most grievous fault,"
beats his boy breast beneath the weight
of a word like *grievous,* guilty of not being
some other boy, one who is not at fault
for being small, though when he kneels erect
he's tall enough. So he never rests his bottom
against his heels, never cheats. Ever. Except
sometimes he does sneak leftover wine
after Mass, savors the *Angelica*—fiery
angel-word—sweet in his mouth and breath.

By 12 he is kneeling for hours in a sanctuary
crowded with a hundred candles and chanting men
in black Benedictine habits, the sweet choke
of incense snaking up the sleeve of his cassock
like the call of vocation rising to his brain.
On the bus, the skin beneath his shirt
coated with holiness like sweat, he
holds his cuff to his nose, inhales
the lingering smoke perfume, walks home
dreaming of gold, light, white, altar,
roses, bells, vowel-starved words
of plaintive Slovak hymns, the Greek *Kyrie*
Lord—he counted 48 notes on one
undulant *melisma* that cost all his breath
on its single-syllable plea—*eleison*
have mercy. It leaves him dizzy,
panting, like a roller coaster makes you
wobble-legged but wanting the more
that the carny promises through curling
cigarette smoke: "As long as you keep screaming, Kid,
you ride for free."

False Gods

Anna, the grandma I never knew, left Slovakia
on the *Stefan Batory* at fifteen. From Chicago,
she wrote home of her suitors: "I'll choose

the kindest eyes." This was Petra, the grandpa
I did know, for a year or two before he died;
the older I get, they say, the more my eyes

grow droopy and gentle as his. I was nine
when the movie *Shane* came out, and idolized
Alan Ladd as did Brandon De Wilde,

the boy, Joey. So at the end—"Shane!
Come back, Shane!"—ashamed, I was crying,
unaware that so was everyone else. It wasn't

just because the rugged cowboy did not
even look back, but because I guessed this
must be some good-for-you kind of thing

only cowboys and grown men understood
and I never would. If there were an 8 millimeter
movie of my nine-year-old life, my dad, like Joey's,

would be mostly busy, away. The flickering film
would show a prematurely sad-eyed little kid
roughhousing with the guy next door, a tall,

curly-headed sailor home from the war. He grabs
a thin wrist and ankle, and spins me like an airplane
until dizzy we tumble into a tickling pile.

Fade to the sailor driving away, hauling a trailer
down 47th Street. I'd like to be digitized, morphed
into that '53 Western so I too could stare

down the road at a hero riding away, never
turning, never waving, so I could cry, "Hey,
Shane! You asshole! What about the kid?"

Gypsy

On Halloween, my shy mother dressed
as a gypsy, as someone who, Grandma said,
you couldn't trust, who in the Old Country
spit in the butter while eyes were turned,
who stole your chickens or even babies.
The dance is in a barn whose tall doors
gape to embrace a wanton moon so large
it tugs the tides in my head. Drums
beat on our bellies, tight as the heads
of tambourines, as we kids run and glide
past the bandstand, slide across the waxed,
sawdusted floor, giddy in our own heat.

Mother's long brown hair, swept up
and off her glowing neck, is caught in silver
combs that shoot a dazzle of stars toward
the eyes of boys not much older than I.
She spins from hand to hand, and layered
skirts—each the shade of an old stain:
red wine on pink satin, coffee on
velvet the color of cream, yellow lace
dipped in crimson—inch up her legs.
She twirls in a blur of ruffles, and I
turn away too late to miss the legs,
long legs, in black silk. Kicking.

Wet Cars

In summer, we boys hung around Dad's car lot
for any chance to touch one, slip inside, rev
an engine. We didn't need to be told twice
to tend to their needs, keep the inventory clean.
Our work clothes, high rubber boots
and cut off jeans—practical for washing cars—
also made the girls stop to admire the wet
machines and our tans, so we'd arc the hose,
make them squeal in the spray, threaten to tell.
When my mother was a girl, she and her sister
once passed a fire house when from an upstairs
window, a fireman doused them with a bucket
of water. They sputter screamed, but didn't run
home, not right away, and didn't tell for years.

Shopping in drizzle-mist for my first car
beneath the glare of haloed bare-bulb stringers,
Dad warns, "Never buy a car in the rain."
Waxed and waterbeaded, even a wreck
can seem all dewy, spangled in sequins,
dazzled in praise. At 17, everything depends
on a red, rain-glazed, candy apple paint job,
on butter-smooth leather upholstery—skin
tanned and sweat-pearled like a Sunday
at the beach where, decked in drying beads
of water light, you and I, just touching,
drift in and out of dreams, but never
out of sight of my car.

Man Making

What it is, when a man works, is hard
hands, cold metal, sweat
red as molten steel
splash, beautiful as a shower of sparks,
as a plowed and planted field
full of fireflies and seed. You work it in,
out, over time, then grab your black lunch pail,
thermos of coffee in the lid, unwrap
your sandwich more bread than meat.

The God who squeezed chaos into light
without getting dirt under his nails,
is up to his elbows in mud making you,
his mouth smeared in first kiss of breath.

"Tell that barber not to wet it,"
Mom warns as I head out the door dreaming
of the day when I would leave the old barber's shop
no longer a boy, but—hair dripping—a man
emerging from the muck, grabbed by the hand,
scrabbling to first feet
brown, wet, naked,
coughing up clay,
ready to get started.

for Gene Bodwin

Swallow

I down a glass of milk
my buddies laced

with pickle juice—a gag
I gulp as though

nothing is wrong,
as if sour and curdled

are to be expected,
begin to believe

that vinegar and gall
will always be

the last swallow,
even when the first

is sweet. I discover
the satisfaction that

bitterness brings,
and the burden

of keeping
this secret.

for Mike Puican

The Naming Of Poles

Father's family was fond of aliases, as if
they'd left Poland on the lam. So Grandpa,
whose namesake I'd be one day, faces
the Ellis Island agent, god-like as Adam
naming beasts (*whatever the man called it,
that would be its name*) thus Wawrzyniec
(the sound of wind rustling through laurel,
the root of Laurence) defeats the likely-Italian
agent horrified at unrelieved consonants,
who dubs him "Lorenzo"—a grand
Polish name.
             Not even immigration
could do much with Grandma. Anna. But
her surname—Róż, a Polish rose, fit
for a maiden's name—at the hands
of pastor and census taker mutates to
Różewska, Rożek, even Jurzenski.

As for their children, Sylvia (really Xaverina
or Zawerka), married an Adams (really
Wroblewski), while the youngest twirled
the Ls of Adele, Adelle, Adelka or sweet
Adeline.
             Meanwhile, Dad was baptized Bolesław,
(really awful in English: Boleslaus)—but
the Polish diminutive is Bolek, easily
anglicized to Bill and formalized to William
which becomes his name—at least until,
dropping everything else, he becomes just Jan
(no rhyme with Don or von) but Jan,
the Used Car Man.
             So Wawrzyniec Lorenzo
Lawrence begat Bolesław Bolek Bill or Jan
who begat me, who begat nobody. I will
come along quietly.

in memory of Chicago poet Mitch Wojtecki

Switchback

after Czesław Miłosz' "Encounter"

Driving east climbing Wyoming's Big Horns,
red-edged wing

of dawn still on the far side
we glimpse grey tarmac unwinding

above us
its dim impossible angles. You whistle. Point. Say

"Thank God that's not *our* way." But it is
the only way,

becoming
exactly what we dread. Where

is our safe
way? Dawn

may expose twists
of plot, but we cannot wait

or turn back, must rush
our beams' reach. I drive hard, not from eagerness

but wonder.

I Have Decided Not To Be...

...this sad city, to have
no crazed citizens

shouting at corner joints
of my bones calling down

doom, begging for change
in the system, not to be

under construction
at every turn, gaping

yellow-taped, orange-coned,
am not an empty subway

car at 3:00 a.m. I have no
weak deep tunnel

arteries, I do not smell
of beef fat and garlic

my high tension
nervewires do not sing

duets with the wet-licked
asphalt like black silk

ripping tirewhines
through the long night

and it is not my endless
thirst draining the lake,

not I sucking in sweet air,
fouling it with my own

Get Your Streetwise!

no thanks
persistent he falls in beside me
up Michigan Avenue, laughs
when my hand draws
my shoulder bag close

I ain't gonna rob you man
no I didn't mean
you probably got a gun in there
what?

still strolling side-by-side

you probably just itchin'
to shoot you a nigger

I stop
he stops I
look him full in the face
into grinning eyes
shake my head walk away defenseless
I
always hold the bag like that
don't want it to slam into people
never touched a gun
can turn it inside out
spill guts on the street
here
look
ungraded papers
poetry books
candy wrappers
look look
pencils
nothing

Listen Carefully

our menu has changed doors
are closing doors will open
on the right black ink is low if
you need help please hang up and
dial operator please don't
lean on the doors please take
the ticket please mind the gap please return
to the clerk with your purchase if you
are a doctor press one if you notice
an unattended package please notify
the authorities we are sorry please try
again surveillance cameras are in use
your behavior may be taped your call
is important to us please turn off
cell phones and pagers we apologize
for any inconvenience
this is a Brown Line train this
is a northbound train this is only
a test this is Joan Rivers reminding you
to buckle up either hang up
or press pound for more
options if this had been an actual emergency
you can be connected at no cost if you
have to wear shoes to walk on the sidewalk
it's the law we expect to be moving again
soon please stand away
from the car your call may be monitored
please take a moment to familiarize yourself
with emergency exits caution
the moving walkway is ending caution
the gate is coming down we continue to be
on highest alert please check your basket we
are experiencing a delay please stand back
please leave a message
spraying is about to begin

Focus

In Omaha, at 53, at 2 in the afternoon,
with no one about, I rolled down a hill.
Samuel Johnson, I've heard, did much
the same at 55, assuring dismayed friends
"I haven't had a roll in a long time."
Without a Boswell to hold my keys
or wallet, I abandon them in a heap
with my glasses and lay on the clover
to wait. Nothing happens.

Like a child who wills himself
too heavy to lift, I must release
my grip, retract roots holding me
in place. Finally, bulge of belly
launches me—a runaway barrel
sloshing on. I lose everything
but speed. Sky flashes at least seven
blue times before my body lay still
again, but laughing, green-stained

with play, dried grass in my beard.
I'd forgotten dizziness, lunch sucked
upward, everything inside loosened.
My ears are eyes that cannot focus.
Only dancers can spin and not grow dizzy,
fix on a single point each time they snap
around, a pulse ahead of falling.

Blues

1.

There's a song so sad, Mama said, *they can't play it*
on the radio. People jump out of windows
when they hear it.
                        It could be true, like when
she'd sing *Put My Little Shoes Away*—a lullaby
about a dying little boy, and I'd cover my ears
and her mouth to stop her—and she'd just nibble
my fingers and laugh.
                        I don't remember how
we got our hands on that record, *Gloomy Sunday,*
but one afternoon Billie Holiday was up there
with me and my buddy Tommy in his tiny attic room,
her voice falling
                        and falling, like tears, three
at a time. We listened hard, one eye on each other
and one on the square light of the one window, waiting
to see if the song really worked.

2.

In '66, at Big John's on Wells in Chicago,
it's three in the morning, Sunday morning, and I
don't know why I'm still here. Everyone I came with

is gone, and Howlin' Wolf is not on stage anymore.
He's crossed the room on his knees, dragging the snake
tail of his mic and now he's kneeling at my table,

at my feet, and I can't tear my eyes away from his,
his cheeks streaked, blue track-shining in the spot,
and I want to touch his round red mouth to stop him

'cause I think he's dying, and I don't know what to do.

Superman's Funeral

Dear Superman,
I'm unhappy that you died. I really missed you. I didn't want you
to die, but you did. I hope you are having fun in heaven. I loved the
movies and cartoons. I wish I can come to your funeral, but I can't
because I live in Chicago.

Sincerely, Dekwante Barber, 5th grade

Superman keeps dying—already three or four times
in my lifetime, Reeve after Reeves crashing the beach
of a boy's imagination, life itself too much, let alone
saving the day for truth, justice, etc. In '93, Doomsday,
a killing machine, lays low the comic book hero, but
it's only a ploy to boost sales, not like in '59, when
a bullet he couldn't outrun, from his own gun, freed him
from TV's pigeon-hole role. And in '95 a fall—
not a tall building, but from a horse, a knight stricken,
and the man of steel is a wheeled man forever—
never-ending battle not withstanding. Ken Kesey's
Superman, Holy Goof Cassady, died in 1969 counting
railroad-tie nails in cold Mexican rain. People expect things
of me, he said, I cannot give. As bad as kryptonite.

I never believed I could fly like the kids you read about
who broke arms and heads plummeting from garage roofs,
flapping towel as useless as broken wings. I had no use
for bending steel or tossing cars around. Claustrophobic
in phone booths, I'd have settled for being Clark Kent:
square-jawed, cleft-chin handsome, shy as I often was,
snappy fedora, horn-rimmed glasses I wished I needed.
That other identity was what I wanted, the secret
every unheroic little guy needs to make himself matter.

Who would guess the Super Man started in Cleveland,
a cartoon brute born of Shuster and Siegel, bespectacled
17 year-old creator gods, shy and gawky with girls.
But the 1931 Depression-depressed country didn't need
another bad buy, wanted swashbucklers in their *Amazing*
Stories and *Weird Tales*, so the boys unbend their guy
into Superman! rippling to save the world—or at least
the good old Uhmerican Way, omnipotence and horny

adolescence wrapped up in one guy easy to miss
in a crowd of two—but with that secret. Girl reporters
of the world don't know that this dull and dopey guy
is the very one they're ga-ga over.
                                                    Sweet.
All it really takes to be a man is a why-chromosome,
being dumb enough not to cry when something hurts,
lucky enough to survive boyhood, and enough testosterone
to fight when someone says you throw like a girl,
or points out that GI Joe really is a doll and you know
in your head that Jimmy Olsen is cuter than Lois Lane.
In the end, even Superman will trip on his own cape, lose
his grip, find kryptonite in his Ovaltine.
                                                    Superman,
I didn't want you to die, but you did and do, and I'll
keep coming to your funeral, even though I live in Chicago,
and probably I'll cry because we're more the same
than I thought. Maybe your hat will fit me now, and since
the old 20/20 is gone, I really do need glasses.

Hope Chest

I could climb inside if I wanted to,
into the cedar breath of what was left
of him, among the tokens he'd sent home
to his new bride: red silk kimono,
a Japanese sword—the scrolled blade
treacherous even to the eye, a Chinese
puzzle box the size of a heart that
could not be pried open by boy fingers,
nor any others I knew. She never saw him
after the war, missing as he was, though
not in action, deserter that he was, but
not of the army. For years she searched
and traced, even saw him once, getting
on a neighborhood bus. When she
admitted in her heart that he just
didn't want to come home, she stopped
looking, but kept the chest and its pungent
gifts, the best, a full-sized parachute.
Even with holes she'd cut for silk kerchiefs,
pillow slips, and baptismal gowns
for neighbors' babies, it still filled, billowed,
when a pal and I ran dragging it down the street
like a kite, shocking drivers who thought
perhaps one of those isolated sentinels—
who'd remained on duty not knowing
the war was over—had heard at last and
dropped from the sky to surprise his sweetheart,
like in the movies. But it was just a couple
of kids being jerked from their feet, tangled
in cedar-smelling silk and cords,
laughing tears smeared with dirty hands.

Found Lost

*If thou wilt be perfect, go and sell that thou hast, and give to
the poor, and thou shalt have treasure in heaven. (Matthew 20: 21)*

When my wallet was found lost (odd expression),
the telephone marathon began, canceling credit
cards, making arrangements—like a dutiful spouse
at my own sudden death. Yet it's only paper lost,
and plastic, not war's scouring, no whirlwind
of fire or earthquake, no flood swirling life's
every sacrament in a vortex, the plug pulled
at the drain end of time. Besides, by noon
I am a citizen again: licensed to spend, drive,
borrow books, a card-carrying member of all
I deem worthy of spent time. I am born again.

When I answer the door, there is no one but
a wallet lying on the stoop. I look for a thread
to tug and tease, but it comes, familiar as an old
brown dog ashamed of where it's spent the night.
Nothing's really gone but currency. I welcome
the thick heft at my hip where it rides again,
lighter for lack of cash, heavier for new secrets,
my old younger and new older faces coexisting
until one expires—a spare identity in case
I get misplaced again. Crossing the threshold, I am
lost again in thought: for a day I'd felt so clean.

Protocol
found at a trail head
Boulder, Colorado Mountain Parks

You are in a mountain lion's home.
Never run, scream, or turn your back.
Make yourself as large as possible; Wave
your arms. Put children
between adults. Speak firmly.
Stand your ground at first,
then slowly back away. If
you're attacked, fight back; Protect
your head and neck. If
you see tracks consider
using another area. We
are fortunate to have
these beautiful creatures.
                              Make noise
as you hike. Wear a bell
if you must hike alone.
Watch your children
and pets carefully. Consider
leaving your pet.

Eager, we lean into the trail
and find within minutes, dead
center in the path, a thigh bone
clean of flesh, moist bits of stained
fur drying in the morning sun.

Suddenly Samson I scout
for an ass's jawbone ready
to snap limbs like pencils,
my body brazen as a bell
tolling above the trail, and
calculate the distance
to the car.

for Bill Mahoney

On Showing Off Your
Seventeen-Year-Old Son
To Your Best Friend Who Has No Kids

I watch your son and you and hate you both
so much that I must leave—saving the scene
on film to torture myself whenever I wish:
the two of you, lawn sprawling, wrestling,
wresting affection with twisting arms, bleats
of pain coughed into laughter—

        he, showing his mother how he bursts
        with all she's fed him;

        you showing her how the old man,
        thin-haired, bellied and wheezing,
        can still pin down her beautiful boy, her baby;

        and you showing me
        up. I know. I know—

I am not there when he maddens you
with his self-centering, do not hear him pout,
clinging to tatters of boyhood, not there
to see you deflate under his disdain. And I
have not tossed away nights in my own house
helpless while a son's rage rises like sap,
swelling, hardening the stem that will snap
and sail him. All I have are these few photos:

        his triumphant grimace squirming out
        from under your equal need to hold him.

Let me tell you something, Dad—you
never had a chance.

for Don and Dan Barshis

Bad Boys

Music's bad boy, rock and roll, jams
through Cleveland's Hall of Fame, blares
from monitors overhead where bearded,
balding men talk and talk about how

it all began. Boys in backturned caps try
to ignore the talking heads who look
so much like their fathers, who in turn
resent being reminded by the flat-bellied

bodies of sons about their own lapsed
youth, already too late to die young. So
father-son pairs talk little, walk not quite
side-by-side: paunched, peach-faced, suited,

pierced: heads bobbing in sync to Pink Floyd,
Morrison, Janis, yet mutually embarrassed, as if
forced to watch a dirty movie together, like
finding out they're in love with the same woman.

for Mike Surufka

28

The Goodbye Kiss

Here it is again:
barging exit of loose-limbed,
chattering boys who stop,
in mid press, for my son
to bend and kiss his dad
goodbye. It's no more
than a brush of lips, but
no mistaking what it is.
He's thirteen.
The day his kisses stop
I will not blame him
since I know a man's dread
of softness, but a boy can't
grow up on his own,
no matter what he thinks.

Again I wonder, is tonight's
the last boy-kiss until I'm
old and harmless, and he's
outgrown conforming he
doesn't even know he needs
as yet? Ashamed, I strained tonight
to hear, beneath the boys'
banter, some taunt to launch
him, to do what his father
isn't man enough to do.

I remember myself, a boy
on a bridge, so high above
a Chicago railyard there was
nothing higher. I backed
into my crouching father,
a fist nestling in a fielder's
glove, then stretched toward
the edge again. He held me
back and spoke so close
I felt his cautions as wind
across my neck, but all
I wanted was to be held
over the edge in his
strong, large hands
and let go.

for Tom Banach

29

Cole DeGenova
Plays The Auditorium Theater

stage hands skew the steinway so we
    cannot see your hands have to watch
        your back black jacket's drape shift right

left shoulder nearly brush your ear humerus
    scapula clavicle—hot percussion trio—hidden
        bones shrug-struggle to burst into wings

fingers work keys unlock what words can
    never—music can only—say your hands play
        ply the great broken-winged black bird coax

from her autumn in new york's slanty crimson light
    long gold purple shadows that sing down and up
        your spine a single humming string

fingers to toes I know a chicago poet when he reads
    out loud he succumbs to his own words can't stop
        tapping out their beat becomes their amplifier

but no mere toe taps for you your legs spread wide
    feet slide in time like plows digging ruts in the stage
        you dance the tune so close we can't tell who's leading

Chicago Cantata

We are Parthians, Medes and Elamites. We live in Mesopotamia,
Judea and Cappadocia . . . yet each of us hears in his own tongue
about the marvels God has accomplished. (Acts 2:9, 11)

Chicago sun burns low in October, still bronze
and brash enough at four o'clock to float
the city's square-shouldered shadows
on the scalloped lake, thick and dark as oil slicks
bubbling up from the sunken well of time.
Massed and proud shapes stretch east,
farther than the towers that cast them are tall,
reach like lovers toward where the morning
has always come. The day's last rays stream
through both window walls of Rockefeller Chapel
leaving the sanctuary air white hot, firing
into one tongue not Parthian, Mede and Elamite,
but Korean, Jew and Indian—adolescent choir
rehearsing Bach, avid for the second coming,
or maybe the first. Hope settles, weighing
what a song weighs, upon the ruffled souls
of passersby hurrying home before the choke
of darkness. *Ich hatte viel Bekümmernis*
in meinem Herzen—I had great distress
in my heart. *Aber deine Troestungen erquicken*
meine Seele—but you refreshed my soul.
In the shadow of the church's bulk, silhouettes
splash through pools of stained light.
A woman stares at the gaping window
where the psalm still overflows. Motionless,
she listens breathing the wet smell of leaves.

March Praise For Global Warming

By now, mid-March, we should be shut of it, but we
who claim to live in Chicago for love

of the hard seasons must now endure what we welcomed
in November. No more squeak

crunch of new snow, merely mounds of ice—worn round-
shouldered as tired Appalachian peaks,

glossed as patent leather and black as fresh-turned earth,
but bearing no seed within, not even

a stone heart. It fell once, the great white leveler, rendered
all things equal, created a strange country

where nothing was defined or called by a name
that you knew, but now we've had enough

of what we once longed to taste, to bury ourselves in, laughing
at its hot sting on our cheeks. What we

stuck out tongues for like holy communion we no longer
desire. It blows about us like ash.

Face Down

When the last black-burnished mound of roadside snow
surrendered, it yielded like receding tide the corpse
of a stuffed toy that lay face down for several days more,
Winnie the Pooh, I think, to judge from yellow bear

body and faded red jacket, though no next of kin
came to claim the remains. Was there a child missing
him, scouring neighborhood alleys, dragging the pool
in the playground? Or had there been an argument?

Had Pooh displeased? deserved getting tossed out
of a passing car or pram, discarded in disgust, or rage?
Maybe he jumped. Why do we let go of what we'd held
so tight, so long that no breath could pass between us?

Maybe we don't let go, but are abandoned, it being better
to lie in mud face down than to be so desperately loved.

Starting Block

Take nothing for your journey, no staff, nor bag, nor bread,
nor money—not even an extra tunic. (Luke 9:3)

After a long, late flight, impatient
to claim my luggage, I allow
my bag to rumble around again
because a battered brown carton
sealed in strapping tape, edges
rounded like an ancient stone,
thumps past, and I know that box.

When I was a boy our family moved
so often we passed through houses
like tourists, abandoned boxes no one
bothered to unpack anymore.
Father called it the 80/20 Law:
"Just twenty percent of what you own
gets almost all your use. The rest,"

he said, "you won't even miss."
The summer we lived along a river
I saw an osprey plummet out of
morning sun to seize a fish
so large its weight alone unclenched
the talons that tucked like landing gear.
He climbed, free again, but hungry.

That box—stuffed with love letters,
china wrapped in yellowed newsprint,
yearbooks signed by girls who dotted
i's with hearts and broke them—bumps by,
and I, ready to dive into time or out, feel
my foot stretch back for something hard,
something steadfast to shove against.

Luminaria

Chicago eats light, sucks it in
like a black hole, hoards it
like a radium dial planning
to stay awake all night because
light—like the grass and flesh
we devour—decays. We
need more. Always. But
unlike broad green leaves
that take their sun straight,
we cannot look full on light
and live. We need the tempering
of angels, moons, or cities
lest we go blind and starve.

But today there's light enough
to squander: towers toy with it,
canyon walls, fluid as melting
sand, play lunch hour catch,
pitch a gleam underhand to brush
against your hair, like a secret stare
in a jammed subway car
that leaves you blushing
and blessed. This city's glass
slabs light your path
in the dark valley. They square off,
gather broken suns
in their thousand panes
to flatter in shadowless
light your unsuspecting face—
you never expect
that single beam to snag
the corner of your eye,
like the glint of a white bird
alight upon your sleeve.

Full Frontal

Invisible ones and naughts of light bounce
off my body standing naked before my brand new
camera, digitally convert to what Burns might call
giftie: "to see oursels as ithers see us!"
though no one sees me so, except in the eyes-off,
locker-room kind of glance, but this
is straight on, dead ahead
                       face blank
as a medical textbook photo—eyes so flat
they may as well be black-barred, bare subject
of some imminent experiment, a mug
waiting to be sentenced.
                   This body
a thick block, barely a difference in girth
between chest and waist, breasts mercifully
not sagging yet—though pencil-line
shadows grin beneath each. Silver hangs
centered on the chest, medal of St. Francis,
where it has been snagging chest hair for decades—
prick of pain only a man can feel.
                   My sex
is barely visible, as if squinting, unused to light
and scrutiny, yet unembarrassed—quite the reverse
of my little-boy dread of being seen naked,
terrorized by schoolyard rumors that in high school
gym class you swim naked! a notion that chilled
like a scrotum in winter, all balls of potential
ascending. Now, much of a lifetime later,
there's no shame left in nakedness, though there are scars—
the only things that do not change.

One, navel to pubis, where I've been recently
opened, flesh peeled back like a tin, in ropey tissue
testifies that hands other than God's have been
messing around inside. Another, barely visible
on my right knee, where I once knelt on alley glass
at the roughhouse hands of Gerald Kasper
when I was seven, recess interrupted by blood spurt,
a nun disinfecting, sending me home to finish bleeding.

Clothing deceives, and in this moment, I am honest,
naked as Allen Ginsberg in his near life-sized photo
once hung in the Art Institute; naked as Jesus
without the loin cloth supplied by artists
whose decorous drapes belied the Romans'
intended last lash of shame but exposed
instead an honest god as one like us.

What makes naked? merely the machines
of sex—cog and gear, tab and slot—unveiled?
If all but these were covered, we'd still be liable
to arrest for exposing ourselves in public,
as if poets were not perpetually naked, pants
always down around our ankles, *in flagrante
delicto*, caught only in compromising positions.

Transfusion

This is still my body, I guess, but this is not
my blood anymore, enriched by two new
units drawn from other arms and hearts
dripping slowly in. Once, boy bloods—
even two or three—might mingle from jabbed
and dirty thumbs pressed to some seal
of faith or trust. But who filled these
plastic sacs, one sucked dry, a second
freshly tapped? No true blue forever friends
I ever knew. I wonder how we will get along.
Maybe the new guys will bully, swagger,

threaten to make some changes around here.
Will I grow taller or fat? Maybe female genes
will render me pregnable, fecund to unimagined
possibility. I worry. Molecules of disease,
I'm assured, are screened out, but what sort
of soul was washed by this blood? What terrors
flushed through whose adrenalin-jolted heart?
What backroads of fatigue mapped whose
bloodshot eyes? What embryo sluiced away?
What sex engorged? What blush bloomed
like sunrise? What bursts of laughter?

Life Studies

1.

Rembrandt scratches his face once again
into copperplate, alters his ego from beggar
to Pontius Pilate who asks us, the crowd, if
we will choose Barabbas or Christ who,
meticulously etched, likewise resembles
the artist. He portrays himself in nearly
a hundred works, less portraiture than
pragmatism at work—not only an at-hand,
cheap model, but the face of rising
celebrity graven into the ready recognition
of prospective buyers. The effect: a world
of a single face in every role, as in dreams
where we are at one time master and slave,
hawk and rabbit. Lover. Demon. Everyone.
No one.

2.

Awaiting Gauguin's arrival, Van Gogh
shaves his head like a monk, paints the
Yellow House full of sunflowers, seminary
for dispatching missionary prophets to convert
the world of art. Instead, drunk on oils and
each other's genius misconstrued, they slump
together into winter. Gauguin's art bursts
from imagination while Van Gogh impastes
only what he sees, can touch—the remains
of brotherhood: their two empty chairs.
Palettes clash, fault lines grind until Vincent
buckles, cracks. So much mad blood thick
upon the stairs; at first Gauguin is suspected
of murder.

Blind Spot

I drive over the brush of years, flatten time
in my wake, scatter leaves in mourning,
one eye on the rearview mirror watching
for ghosts who refuse to be left behind and stalk
like state troopers waiting for any excuse
to pull me over, blue lights screaming. I can't
speed up and can't get out of the way of what
is always, always closer than it seems.

My six-year-old niece, pondering death
for the first time at her great-grandfather's
wake is told, "No, Honey. We can't take
Papa home with us in the car!" I'm laughing
over this with my brother until he adds that she,
grasping that it is the old who tend to die,
cried "But Grandma and Grandpa are old!"—

our own elderly parents, and I'm blindsided
again by the unthinkable I think of every day,
roaring up from nowhere. Gaining. It isn't fair
for a little kid who can't even drive to glare
mortality's high-beam in my rearview mirror
when I'm trying to be so damned careful
not to collide with what's right in front of me.

No Hold Barred

I remember the friend who cannot make a point
without touching my sleeve, another who easily
drapes my shoulder with his arm, the groom—
full of his wedding day—who thanks me, his priest,
for the ceremony and my friendship, walks me
to my car across the broad lawn, his hand
unselfconsciously holding mine, a welding
of men. When my barber shampoos my hair I am
most aware that days and weeks have passed
with no one having touched me and I do not
want him to stop. Most men block the threat
of embrace with stiff handshake, would never
hold another man except in sweat of triumph
or grief. How unlike my brother who never hugs
for mere seconds at our infrequent meetings,
but holds on, as if to what is easily lost, his grip
even longer than the yogi who insists a hug
should last for three breaths—two too long.

for Gabriel Halpern

The Adventures Of A Poem
Lost On The Way To An Open Mic

On Dearborn Street a sheet of 24 lb.
bond blown out of my hand, flutters,
slaps up against a steamy plate glass
window as the poets inside are pouring out
words like aphrodisiacal tea or heavy
oil to lubricate the knots of love.
Before I can grab them, my poems
catch the night wind like a sail.
Speechless, I hunker in the doorway,
watch all I meant to say fly away.

I imagine a woman blocks, miles
away finding the page pasted with rain
to her front door. She peels it away
like litter, dismisses it with as little regard
as you pay to flyers shoved into your hand
good for a discount visit to a massage parlor
or a free ticket to a TV game show.
                                        Aloft again,
my poem—planned for slamming
poetical ears—is lifted by the hawk
hunting for someone to stun
with words: that in-the-middle-of-your-gut
Amen moan, grunt of Yes, I know
that same shame, shudder, bliss, rage!
or maybe the page,
or just a word torn from it, will be stuffed
into a wallet, stuck to a mirror,
or in a mind, and taken for a ride.
                                        Maybe
it will be found barely alive,
a fallen bird lifted to the breast
pocket of a young boy who
will leave his play to nurse its weak pulse
just because it is lost and out of breath. He
will keep it in a cardboard box beside his bed,
a hot water bottle and ticking clock
wrapped in a towel to trick it
into staying alive. But soon the boy
will learn that a poem must outlive

its paper, to survive in the wild air.
So he will begin to whisper and sing
in new words of his own—and having it
by heart by now, he will crease my poem
into a single wing, throw open his window,
send it soaring.

Adam And Eve On Halsted Street

Nothing to distinguish these two from dozens
of cute couples on this first warm night in April,

young, it's true, but so is everyone else.
Beautiful? Yes, it must be said, but not

fit for the face-peddlers, more like the rest of us
than not. Unselfconscious, they could be

the last two of us all, or the first ever
to cross this street into the ever-under-construction

future. This is Boys Town, Chicago,
girls in pairs, boys holding hands common

as loaded grocery bags or a pair
of six packs dangling in either hand,

the look of Friday night in every eye—that easy,
desperate hunger for someone. Here in the largesse

of this city, there's plenty of room at the table
or on the sidewalk even for a boy-and-girl pair,

perfect as clear writing on two sides of a page:
one story impossible to tell without the other,

unaware that they live now in a poem
as a primal paradigm, a pair sacred—not

because of some God-imputed law for how
to couple—but just for their blessed halfness.

Neruda Raises Questions

Tell me, is the rose naked
or is that her only dress?
          Pablo Neruda, The Book of Questions

Diga me: Why
is the only question God needs
to answer, but I
have many to ask:

Was it not devilish of God
to plant a tree right here,
in the goddamned (sorry)
middle of the garden,

lovely to look at,
exquisite for nibbling
at knowledge
of good and evil?

The smallest bite
is dangerous, but so is
hunger. How shall you live
without asking?

Present Perfect

There is no today where I am. New
or now may show up tomorrow, but
my money's on yesterday's parade
of *mights* and *should haves*.

Who could have predicted that I
would become a dumb plumb line
marking *was* as true and *used to be*
as better than *is*, even though *I know*

was was worse. When a mercy
morning burns away like fog,
there follow noon and still-livid
scars—I thought I was loving you—so

how can any be a better day,
or tomorrow? Nepenthe, goddess
or drug, allayer of pain, soother
of old sorrows, does not exist.

If I knew where to lay my hands on
common rue, I'd swallow its flower
whole, wash it down with sour
wine—I have not done with dregs.

White Wolf On Red Harley

as if lobo could not lope

fast enough   had devoured
some biker whole

and in such rush
wolf grew wheels   shape shifted

by wind   wrapped in white
hide   its head a helmet

rainshining blackjewel snout
pointing ahead   ears twitchprick

to a brother beyond traffic
howl   dead glass eyes stare

down the lead October sky   skin sleeves
throttle-cranking paws

fur draped like a wedding dress
white veil flying

     I should have followed

What Celibacy Is

. . . And there be eunuchs which have made themselves eunuchs for the kingdom of heaven's sake. He that is able to receive it, let him receive it. (Matthew 19:12)

If this is what
it costs to hold
at heart a hollow
where no sparrow
lives (nothing alive
that needs light),

if this is what God
expects from Yes,
then it is too much
today, although
I pay it anyway.
Again. Some heroic

souls, though few,
I expect, accept
such terms without
complaint: those
who, full of You
to breaking, can

cut off every
other thing and
one, swallow
pain like wine,
smiling, drugged
on purest Spirit,

proof that You
exist, the mere dregs
of You enough
to feel or fill
another day. But
this hole in me

is not wholly
holy yet (if ever
it will be), is still
child-round and
lover-shaped
by someone as like

yet utterly unlike
me as I am like
and utterly other
than You, who
haunt and echo-
ache in that space

You claim
to hallow, but
which feels
merely hollow.
Will I now
meet You here?

Incarnation

*The Lord will dance over you with gladness, and
renew you in his love. (Zephaniah 3:17)*

I am with you. Here,
not there, not even
near. Here. Breath
could not be closer
nor hot blood pulse.

I am with you, not
leaving, promising
one day to return, but
here. Now. Dance
with me, your head

on my shoulder as when
your father danced you
asleep to Glenn Miller
records at two a.m.
You are not a baby

now, nor boy. A man.
I know. Now dance,
your arms around me.
Grab my sweater
with both hands.
Dance.

Doxology

Vivas to those who have failed!
Walt Whitman

All praise for all
who cannot walk barefoot in grass
or leap to avoid a shard of glass

in time; Praise
for those who cannot smell boxwood,
bread, or sweat. Praise too for those

who cannot taste sweet
water cold and hard enough to hurt
your teeth. Praise for those who've

never watched a baby
trace the curl of a cat's tail, nor
back-brushed the patterned mail

of a snake's skin. All praise
for those who've never galloped
bareback on the *gigue* of Bach's

First Cello Suite, nor
danced a grass-stained-finger-stinging
barehanded catch. Praise for those

who no longer remember the words
to "You Are My Sunshine,"
nor sing their own praises,

who find no reason to.
Glory, honor and power for them:
praise and every blessing.

Year Of Grace

What you do on New Year's day, Grandpa used to say,
you'll do every day of the coming year. Great. A year
of waking every morning at 2:58 loathing your flaws,
dozing only to jolt with alarm barely in time to pray
distracted by sour sins, a misaligned spine, and promise—
again—fidelity to God and yoga, wondering what
promises will cost
      breakfast regret over last night's
New Year's Eve dinner: charred bruschetta abandoned
to smoulder on the porch and bloody chicken:
nothing to eat but baked potatoes—and only two
of those between us because one blew up in the oven—
and peas
   so
     every day you'll shower, trim your beard
(should you just let it go grey?) gulp vitamins,
more coffee, then send a poem to a friend helpless
in the face of his mother's diminishing, out to mail it
and return rented films wondering at how much time
you waste watching what isn't real—people, love,
not even lust—yet you do watch, which isn't the same
as paying attention,
     then
       a long walk in awe of winter's
zeal for propelling us into each other's arms,
in awe of that couple's oblivion to everything
except their ice breath blend of fog kisses, and
you ask yourself what you're doing wrong, why
you are alone, why you mostly love people who have
other people to love them
     so
      it looks like every day this year
you'll haunt bookstores and coffee bars to write in,
suck espresso in spite of which you'll doze
over some scribble-tail ramble of a poem to dream
of a beautiful stranger serving coffee naked
then jerk awake to un-celibate thoughts
as the batteries in your CD player die
letting you hear that Billie Holliday's been singing
Gershwin lyrics that somehow you've known
from the womb *songs of love, but not for me*—until
it's time for you and your self-pity to go home,
      but first,

you browse the poetry section, visualize
your own name on a book spine—shelved between
Ignatow and Jarrell—ah! Sweet Bitterness:
to be remaindered! begin to suspect that, even if
this is the year your book gets published, it will have
a shitty cover, and on the way home, you rent another movie
you probably won't watch,

             and

                  remember all the friends
you've promised to pray for every day but so far today
you haven't—so for miles along Lake Shore Drive—
windows rolled down—Bill and Tom and Susan,
Ann Marie and Richard each face looming bright,
haloed in your breath like rising moons, a ripple
of angels,

       and

         when you get home, the apartment
is empty and dark, and you promise yourself
to organize your mess of a desk, and wonder why
there is so much waste in the life you keep living,
loving, and losing control of, make macaroni
and cheese from a box doctored with the chicken—
cooked at last—and while you watch the news
a mousetrap snaps in the kitchen, and you blush
at your distinctly un-Franciscan satisfaction

                and
at 7 p.m., a church basement meeting where you
remember, again, what it used to be like,
what happened, and what it's like now,
how God is doing for you what you could never do
for yourself—which is most things—and hug
a dozen beautiful human beings and wish them all
a happy new year

About the Author

Larry Janowski is a native Chicagoan, son of a used car dealer, a teacher, short story writer, poet, and real-life Friar Lawrence. He began his professional writing career as a reporter and editor with the Associated Press. A thorough Midwesterner, Larry grew up on the South Side of Chicago, went away to prep school in Wisconsin, got his BA back in Chicago at the University of Illinois, went to grad school at the University of Wisconsin in Madison, and seminary at Aquinas Institute of Theology in Dubuque, Iowa. Only his MFA is from out east: Vermont College. He joined the Franciscans in 1968, and was ordained in 1973.

He has won prizes in fiction (*The Critic, Praying Magazine*) and poetry at *Literal Latté* ("Gypsy" chosen by Cornelius Eady) and *River Oak Review*. He's received development grants from the state of Wisconsin and city of Chicago, a residency at The Blue Mountain Center, and the J.R.H. Moorman Scholarship at St. Deiniol's Residential Library in Great Britain. He has published two chapbooks: *Chicago Cantata* (2001) and *Celibate Dazzled* (2003). Janowski is an adjunct professor of English at Dominican University and at Wilbur Wright Community College where he was named the City Colleges of Chicago Distinguished Part Time Professor 2001-2002.

After living and working for almost 30 years in southeastern Wisconsin, Larry returned to Chicago in 1995, still madly in love with the city, its people and skyline, its music and noise, its art and style, its poetry.

Acknowledgments

Many of these poems have appeared (sometimes in other versions) in *After Hours: a Journal of Chicago Writing and Art, BlackWater Review, The Critic, Court Green, First Things, The Heartlands Today, Literal Latté, Paterson Literary Review, Rhino, River Oak Review, Spoon River Poetry Review, Trail and Timberline,* and *TriQuarterly,* and *Celibate Dazzled* (Franciscan University Press, 2003).

Thanks to the City of Chicago Department of Cultural Affairs and the Blue Mountain Arts Center for time and support in writing these poems, and to the following poets: Reginald Gibbons, Edward Hirsch, Paul Mariani, William Olsen, Betsy Sholl and Barry Silesky. Special acknowledgment to fellow South Sider Stuart Dybek for his early and ongoing encouragement, and to Dave Isay, Lloyd Newman, and LeAlan Jones, whose radio story "Remorse: The 14 stories of Eric Morse" inspired me to finish the title poem.

I am especially grateful to Chris Green and Tony Trigilio and to Jan Bottiglieri, Nina Corwin and Brenda Cárdenas–amazing poets all. Special thanks and acknowledgment to Al DeGenova and Patricia Hertel, editors of *After Hours*—an outstanding journal where many of these poems first found a home. Thank you to editor and publisher David Gecic who *is* Puddin'head Press, and to Bill Mahoney for the generous back cover photo.

Finally, I am grateful to my Franciscan brothers who have kept me from falling for my own publicity, and most of all to *brothers* Bill Mahoney and Kent Matthies who just keep me from falling.

The Puddin'head Press also carries titles from other
publishing concerns including:

FRACTAL EDGE PRESS
Old Gloves by Beatriz Badikian
Black On White by Beyond The M.C.
What Stone Is By Michael Brownstein by Michael Brownstein
Elegy For James Gerard and Other Poems by Daniel Cleary
Blood, Sex, & Prayer by Jim Coppoc
I Am Spam by Larry O. Dean
A Fine Line by Maureen Flannery
The Urban Poems by David Hernandez
In The Warhouse by Reginold Gibbons
Decades Of Rehearsal by Wayne Allen Jones
Stoneworks by Wayne Allen Jones
The A-Poems by Jones And Mccabe
Marginal State by Francesco Levato
Marriage Bones by Lauren Levato
The Reprehensibles by Gary Lilley
Dis; Voices From A Shelter by Ray McNiece
Us? Talking Across America by Ray McNiece
Dead Machine City by Charlie Newman
Words by Charlie Newman
Hosts At Trace by Polyrhythmic Collective
Choruses One by Joe Roarty
Griever's Circuit by Thomas Roby
The Suburban Poems by John Starrs
Conscience Under Pressure by Billy Tuggle
Shooting Dead Films With Poets by Lina Vitkanskas

LAKE SHORE PUBLISHING
The Talking Poems: A Family Legend by Anne Brashler
Yes, No Maybe by Glen Brown
I've Been Away So Many Lives by Richard Calish
Sit By Me by Edith Freund
Next Year Country by Louise Liffengren Hullinger
From The Foxes Den by Priscilla A. Johnson
Why Horses, Mrs. K by Blanche Whitney Kloman
Times Rides The River by Robert Mills
Oils Of Evening by G.E. Murray
Soundings: A Poetry Anthology by Carol Spelius
Aqueus And Other Tales by Carol Spelius
How We Got Here From There by Carol Spelius
I, Mancha by Carol Spelius

OMMATION PRESS
Poems From The Body Bag by Michael Brownstein
Cheap Entertainment by Liz Leblanc
No Mean Feet by Liz Leblanc
Languid Love Lyrics by Effie Mihopoulos
The Mooncycle by Effie Mihopoulos

OTHER PUBLICATIONS

Mapmaker Revisited by Beatrice Badikian
Woman Of My Dreams by David Barr
Hack by Robert Boone
A Period Of Trees by Michael Brownstein
Breaking Into The Safe Of Life by Susan Cherry
The Green Ribbon by Daniel Cleary
On The Root River Trail by Daniel Cleary
Back Beat by Al DeGenova And Charles Rossiter
Oceans And Landmass by Scott Dekatch
Talking Around Reason by Scott Dekatch
The Music Of Solid Objects by John Dickson
Waving At Trains by John Dickson
Avalance Expert by Shelia Donahue
Cook County Forest Preserves by William Eiden
Departures by Robert Klein Engler
One Hundred Poems by Robert Klein Engler
Ancestors In The Landscape by Maureen Flannery
Secret Of The Rising Up by Maureen Flannery
The Science Of Broken People by Todd Heldt
Satin City Serenade by David Hernandez
License To Quill by C. J. Laity
Verbal Paint by Nicole Macaluso
Debris by Elizabeth Marino
Street Preachers, Hookers, And Other Martyrs by John Martinez
Recipe For Disaster by Pamela Miller
Bent Out Of Shape by Joanne Ortman
Faith 2 Talk by Kayleah Jewel Porter
A Beating Of Wings by Gertrude Rubin
Wanderlust by Maggie Rubin
Seven Minutes Before The Bombs Drop by Jared Smith
Walking The Perimeter Of The Plate Glass Window Factory by Jared Smith
Seeing My Mother Off And Other Poems by Adam Swinford-Wasem
Shakespeare's Funky Love Cats by Bruce Tate
A Dozen Cold Ones by E. Donald Two-Rivers
Pow Wows, Fat Cats, and Other Indian Tales by E. Donald Two Rivers
Cinnabar by Martha Modena Vertreace
Dragon Lady: Tsukimi by Martha Modena Vertreace
Glacier Fire by Martha Modena Vertreace
Light Caught Bending by Martha Modena Vertreace
Maafa: When Night Becomes A Lion by Martha Modena Vertreace
Oracle Bones by Martha Modena Vertreace
Second House From The Corner by Martha Modena Vertreace
Second Mourning by Martha Modena Vertreace
Smokeless Flame by Martha Modena Vertreace
Caged Birds by Constance Vogel
The Mulberry by Constance Vogel
Rosedust by Larry Winfield
Chicago Poetry Fest 2004 Anthology
Chicago Poetry Fest 2005 Anthology
And
AFTERHOURS Magazine

THE PUDDIN'HEAD PRESS

Publisher and distributor of fine books

CURRENT TITLES

ORDINARY by Carol Anderson
THROUGH MY EYES by Samuel Blechman
INSIDE JOB by Robert Boone
CONVERSATIONS WITH FRIENDLY DEMONS
AND TAINTED SAINTS by Nina Corwin
LAKE MICHIGAN SCROLLS by John Dickson
I'M NOT TONIGHT by Kris Darlington
LADY RUTHERFURD'S CAULIFLOWER by JJ Jameson
THE LAUNDROMAT GIRL by Lee Kitzis
CHICAGO PHOENIX by Cathleen Schandelmeier
LAKE MICHIGAN AND OTHER
POEMS by Jared Smith
PROPHECIES by Lawrence Tyler
THE ANTI-MENSCH ANTHOLOGY
THE ANTI-MENSCH II ANTHOLOGY
STARWALLPAPER STUDENT ANTHOLOGY

Published by Puddin'head Press and Collage Press

THRESHOLDS by Jeff Helgeson
CROWDPLEASER by Marc Smith
LESSONS OF WATER AND THIRST by Richard Fammeree

For more information and a complete catalog contact us:

Puddin'head Press
P. O. Box 477889
Chicago IL 60647
(708) 656-4900
(888) BOOKS-98 (orders only)

www.puddinheadpress.com
phbooks@compuserve.com